EARTH, SPACE, AND BEYOND

# WHAT DOES
# SPACE EXPLORATION
# DO FOR US?

Neil Morris

Chicago, Illinois

**www.heinemannraintree.com**
Visit our website to find out
more information about
Heinemann-Raintree books.

**To order:**

☎ Phone 888-454-2279

💻 Visit www.heinemannraintree.com
to browse our catalog and order online.

Edited by Andrew Farrow, Adam Miller and Adrian
Vigliano
Designed by Marcus Bell
Original illustrations ©Capstone Global Library 2011
Illustrated by KJA-artists.com
Picture research by Hannah Taylor
Originated by Capstone Global Library Ltd.
Printed in China by South China Printing Company, Ltd.
15 14 13 12 11
10 9 8 7 6 5 4 3 2 1

**Library of Congress Cataloging-in-Publication Data**
Morris, Neil, 1946-
  What does space exploration do for us? / Neil Morris.
    p. cm.—(Earth, space & beyond)
  Includes bibliographical references and index.
  ISBN 978-1-4109-4159-6 (hc)—ISBN 978-1-4109-4165-
7 (pb) 1. Astronautics—International cooperation—
Juvenile literature. 2. Outer space—Exploration—Juvenile
literature. 3. Astronautics I. Title.
  TL788.4.M676 2012
  629.4—dc22            2010040159

**Acknowledgments**
The author and publishers are grateful to the following
for permission to reproduce copyright material: Corbis
pp. 5 (©epa),10, 15 (©Science Faction/ Peter Ginter), 17
(©Gene Blevins/LA Daily News), 30 (©Julie Dermansky),
35 (©Reuters); ©Dynamic Systems, Inc p. 23; Getty
Images pp. 20 (Photographer's Choice/ Peter Dazeley),
25 (Science Faction/ Jim Sugar), 38 (AFP); NASA pp. 11,
14 (MSFC/D. Higginbotham), 7, 8, 9 (Marshall Space
Flight Center [MSFC]), 10 inset (JPL-Caltech), 13, 18, 19
(Lawrence Ong), 22, 24 (Johnson Space Center), 26, 27
(European Space Agency), 29 (Johnson Space Center),
32 (Kim Shiflett), 33 (Tony Landis), 34, 36 (Orbital
Debris Program Office), 37, 39; Photolibrary p. 21
(©Fotosearch); Science Photo Library pp. 4 (©European
Southern Observatory), 6 (©NASA), 12 (©Michael
Dunning), 16 (©Pascal Goetgheluck), 31 (©NASA), 40
(©Dr Seth Shostak).

Cover photograph of Jodrell bank radio telescope
reproduced with permission of Science Photo Library
(©David Parker).

We would like to thank Professor George W. Fraser for his
invaluable help in the preparation of this book.

# EARTH, SPACE, AND BEYOND

## WHAT DOES SPACE EXPLORATION DO FOR US?

# Contents

Some words are shown in bold, **like this**. You can find out what they mean by looking in the glossary. You can also look out for them in the "Word Station" box at the bottom of each page.

# Space Achievements

Many people see space exploration as one of the greatest challenges facing humanity. Exploring our **Universe** has led to extraordinary achievements, along with many failures. The successes have brought enormous benefits. In this book we will take a close look at the advantages and disadvantages of exploring space. The information will help you come to your own conclusion about what space exploration really does for us.

## What is space?

Space is the whole of the Universe that lies beyond Earth's **atmosphere**. It is sometimes called outer space, because it is outside, or beyond, our planet. Before humans started exploring space, they knew where it started – in the sky. But where does it end and how big is it? These are questions that **astronomers** have been trying to answer for centuries.

This region of stars, gas, and dust lies in a faraway galaxy. The dramatic photograph was taken using a powerful telescope in Chile.

One of the two 8.4-meter- (27.6-foot-) wide mirrors that collect light in the Large Binocular Telescope. This large instrument lies at 3,221 meters (10,567 feet) above sea level.

## Ancient astronomy

Scientists in the ancient world studied the night skies and learned a great deal about the Universe. They realized that their increasing knowledge had practical benefits, such as marking-out time, and making clocks and calendars. Their understanding of the Sun and stars also helped farmers set the best times for planting and harvesting crops. In the 5th century BCE, the Greek mathematician and astronomer Oenopides discovered that the Earth is tilted as it spins. He believed that the tilt angle was 24° and he was very close. Later astronomers calculated the tilt more accurately at 23.44°. Because the tilt moves us towards and away from the Sun, this tilt causes our seasons.

## Telescopes

Astronomers such as Galileo first used **telescopes** at the beginning of the 17th century. Galileo's small device showed him that the Moon was not smooth, as people had thought, but covered in hills and craters. Since then, engineers have made telescopes bigger and more powerful. Some are even sent up into space. One of the largest Earth-based telescopes is the Large Binocular Telescope, on Mount Graham in Arizona, which is funded by German and Italian institutes as well as the United States.

### The Space Age

The Space Age can be said to have begun on October 4, 1957, when the Soviet Union sent the first artificial **satellite** into **orbit** around the Earth. Named Sputnik (Russian for "satellite"), it circled the Earth once every 96 minutes. The satellite transmitted radio signals that amateur radio users picked up with great excitement all over the world.

## Escaping the pull of the Earth

In the 20th century, scientists realized that they needed a very powerful launch vehicle to send anything into space. Otherwise, Earth's **gravity** would pull any spaceship back to Earth. The answer was a huge rocket, which burned fuel to make hot gases that rushed out through a nozzle at the back. Scientists discovered that to carry a satellite into orbit around Earth, a rocket had to speed up to about 27,000 kilometers per hour (16,777 miles per hour). The rocket that carried Sputnik (the first artificial satellite) was 30 meters (98 feet) long.

An enormous Saturn-V rocket lifts-off in 1969 to send the *Apollo 11* spacecraft on its journey to the Moon. The thin rocket at the top is a launch escape system for use in an emergency. Saturn-V had a total of 11 engines in 3 stages.

This artist's impression shows an Apollo spaceship (left) docking with *Soyuz-19* in 1975. Three U.S. astronauts and two Soviet cosmonauts visited both country's spacecraft.

## Space race

On April 12, 1961, Soviet cosmonaut (Russian for "astronaut") Yuri Gagarin became the first human in space. U.S. astronaut Alan Shepard followed him into space less than four weeks later. This was the beginning of the "space race" between the world's two most powerful nations. In 1968, U.S. *Apollo 8* became the first spaceship with a human crew to orbit the Moon. The following year, on July 20th, Neil Armstrong stepped out of the lunar module of *Apollo 11* to become the first human to set foot on the Moon. This did not end the rivalry, but by 1975 the two nations cooperated with each other as an Apollo spaceship joined up with a Russian Soyuz spaceship 225 kilometers (140 miles) above the Earth.

## Aiming for the Moon

U.S. President John F. Kennedy said in a famous speech in 1961: "I believe that this nation should commit itself to achieving the goal, before this decade is out, of landing a man on the Moon and returning him safely to the Earth." This was an amazing statement, made just twenty days after the first American was launched into space. A Moon shot needed an even more powerful rocket that could reach a speed of 40,000 kilometers per hour (24,854 miles per hour). Seven years after President Kennedy's statement, a 111-meter- (364-foot-) long Saturn-V rocket sent astronauts into orbit around the Moon. (See the box at right for more on this.)

## A new challenge

One of the greatest problems of space exploration is cost. Engineers realized that it was an expensive waste to use a spaceship just once, so in the 1970s they started work on building a reusable spaceship. The U.S. space shuttle program began in 1972, and in 1981 the *Columbia* shuttle blasted off into space and returned safely to Earth. Seven months later *Columbia* made its second space flight.

WORD STATION
*gravity* force that attracts things towards the center of Earth (or another planet, star, or galaxy)

## Living in space

Many scientists have wanted to know if it is possible for astronauts to live in space for a lengthy period of time. This will be essential if humans want to travel to distant stars and planets. To test this, engineers began designing space stations. These are large spaceships, which can serve as a space hotel, laboratory, and observatory. The Soviets sent up the first space station, Salyut, in 1971. Two years later the U.S. Skylab followed. Further stations followed, until the United States and Russia joined forces with other nations in 1993 to start building an International Space Station.

## Health and safety

Space exploration has taught us a lot about the effects of weightlessness on human muscles and bones. In the weightless and cramped conditions of a spaceship, astronauts' muscles weaken and shrink. This also applies to the muscular organ that pumps blood around the body, the heart. So astronauts exercise while they are in space, using special machines. These help muscles and bones, but medical researchers have found that astronauts' bones still lose one percent of density every month they spend in space. This density is the amount of minerals and other substances that work to keep bones strong and healthy.

A U.S. scientist studies a checklist as he tests an exercise machine aboard the International Space Station. He wears special tights fitted with sensors.

## Observing space from space

Ever since the telescope was invented, astronomers have searched for ways of reducing the distorting effects of the Earth's atmosphere on their views of space. In the 20$^{th}$ century space scientists achieved this by sending a telescope beyond Earth's atmosphere. They named the world's first space telescope after the U.S. astronomer Edwin Hubble, who used giant telescopes to study faraway **galaxies**. In 1990, NASA launched the Hubble Space Telescope aboard a space shuttle and sent it into orbit 569 kilometers (353 miles) above the Earth. Unfortunately there was a tiny fault in the telescope's main light-gathering mirror, which spoiled early images. But shuttle astronauts repaired the mirror three years later.

### Overcoming space telescope problems

"Over the years, Hubble has suffered broken equipment, a bleary-eyed primary mirror, and the cancellation of a planned shuttle servicing mission. But the ingenuity and dedication of Hubble scientists, engineers, and NASA astronauts allowed the observatory to rebound and thrive. The telescope's crisp vision continues to challenge scientists and the public with new discoveries and evocative images."

**NASA, 2010**

An astronaut on space shuttle *Endeavour* prepares to make a repair to the Hubble Space Telescope. The photograph also captures a wonderful image of Earth.

*galaxy* group of billions of stars, gas, and dust bound together by gravity

# Understanding the Universe

Space exploration has taught us a lot about astronomy, the scientific study of the Universe. In 1962, just five years after the launch of the first satellite, a space probe flew close to another planet. This was the U.S. probe Mariner-2, which traveled through space for more than three months to get close to Earth's nearest planetary neighbor, Venus.

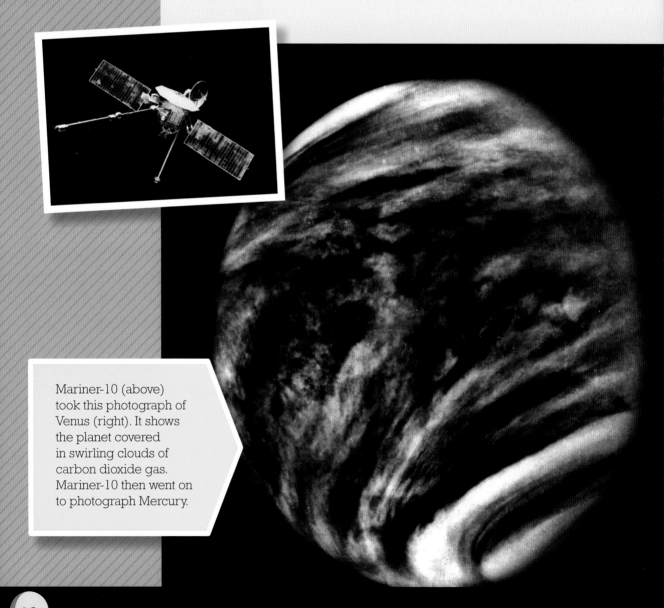

Mariner-10 (above) took this photograph of Venus (right). It shows the planet covered in swirling clouds of carbon dioxide gas. Mariner-10 then went on to photograph Mercury.

## Learning at close quarters

Before space travel the other planets in our **solar system** were unknown quantities. Ancient astronomers observed Venus, but until 1962 we knew little about the planet's structure. Then in 1970, a Soviet Venera-7 spaceship landed on Venus, and four years later the U.S. probe Mariner-10 sent the first close-up photographs of the planet. These and other early space probes told scientists that Venus had an atmosphere made up mainly of carbon dioxide, with a surface temperature of 475°C (887°F). These facts could never have been discovered from Earth.

## From 1682 to 2061

In 1682, the English astronomer Edmund Halley observed a **comet** that was later named "Halley's Comet" after him. He calculated that the comet would appear every 76 years, and it did appear again in 1758, after his death. In 1986, the European Space Agency (ESA) probe Giotto flew through the comet's **coma** (a cloud of dust and gas surrounding the comet) and photographed its **nucleus** (center).

Experts did not expect the spaceship to survive its battering from comet dust, but most of its instruments remained operational. This meant that astronomers learned a huge amount about what comets are made of. Photographs showed the comet's nucleus to be about 15 kilometers (9 miles) long and 7–10 kilometers (4-6 miles) wide. Later analysis of the data confirmed that the comet formed about 4.6 billion years ago. It will be visible again from Earth in the year 2061.

### Far side of the Moon

When we look at the Moon, we always see the same near side of its globe. This is because the Moon spins once during each trip around Earth. Before October 7, 1959, no one had seen the far side of the Moon. Then a Soviet Luna-3 space probe orbited the Moon and sent back photographs of the far side. Eight years later, three U.S. astronauts became the first humans to view the far side directly when *Apollo 8* flew around the Moon. While the spaceship was behind the Moon, it was out of radio contact with the Earth. There was an anxious wait in mission control until the craft reappeared.

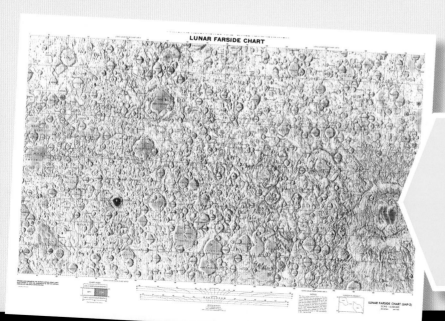

LUNAR FARSIDE CHART

NASA used photographs taken from spacecraft to make this detailed chart of the far side of the Moon. Before 1959 astronomers could not be certain about what the unseen side looked like.

## Past, present, and future

The more we explore space, the more we know about the Universe and understand our planet's place in it. Most scientists believe that the Universe began with a massive explosion known as the **Big Bang**. They also believe that the Universe is still expanding. This means that as we look further out into space, we are looking back in time. The more we understand the history of the Universe, the more we can know the present and predict the future. Some scientists believe that eventually the Universe might stop expanding and collapse to nothing again. This theory is known as the **Big Crunch**.

An artist's impression of the Big Bang. Scientists believe the Universe started this way about 13.5 billion years ago.

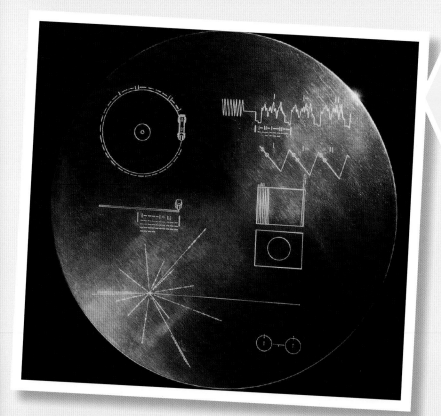

The Voyager spacecraft contain gold-plated disks with sounds and images of Earth. The cover (seen here) shows how the disk is played and describes the location of our Sun.

## Traveling beyond the solar system

Voyagers 1 and 2, both spaceships without people on board, were launched in 1977. They made important discoveries about volcanoes on Jupiter's moon Io and details of Saturn's rings. Voyager-2 then went on to explore Uranus and Neptune, before both spaceships left the solar system. In 2010, Voyager 1 was 17 billion kilometers (10.6 billion miles) and Voyager 2 just short of 14 billion kilometers (8.7 billion miles) from the Sun. More than 30 years after they left our planet, both spaceships continue to send back data to scientists on Earth.

## Alien life on Titan?

Scientific findings are open to different interpretations, and space reports can be confusing or even misleading. On June 5, 2010 the British newspaper *The Daily Telegraph* titled an article: "Titan: NASA scientists discover evidence 'that alien life exists on Saturn's moon'." The article stated: "Researchers at the space agency believe they have discovered vital clues that appeared to indicate that primitive aliens could be living on the moon [Titan]." But the original NASA article quoted two papers that simply stated that some scientists believe there could be some form of "primitive methane-based life" on Saturn's moon. To clear things up, the NASA scientist quoted in the original article wrote, "This is still a long way from 'evidence of life'." Are you confused yet? This shows how theories and ideas can be turned into "facts" by eager newspaper editors looking for attention-grabbing stories about aliens!

A solar sail is made of a very thin plastic material that contains solar cells. The Sun's energy pushes the sail through space.

## Energy from our local star

Through space research we have also learned a lot about energy and how to use it. All Earth's energy comes from the Sun, our nearest star. Increased knowledge has helped us use its power more sensibly. Several space probes have been launched to study the Sun closely, including a Japanese probe named Hinode ("Sunrise" in Japanese). Another Japanese spaceship called Ikaros (Interplanetary Kite-craft Accelerated by Radiation of the Sun) uses the latest solar sail technology to move through space using only the power of the Sun. This "space yacht" tells us even more about solar energy as it uses it to make its way towards Venus.

## Learning from the Sun

Human-made nuclear reactors use nuclear fission — the splitting of atoms — rather than **fusion** (see the panel at right). In 2003, China and South Korea joined a group consisting of the European Union, Japan, Russia, and the United States to work together on a nuclear fusion project based in France. India joined the group in 2005. Called ITER (International Thermonuclear Experimental Reactor), the project aims to produce a reactor that will lead to a full-scale nuclear-fusion power plant by 2026 or 2027.

## Infrared future?

Nearly half of the Sun's radiation is in the form of **infrared** rays, which we feel on Earth as heat. Most of the other half is visible radiation, or light. The U.S. and European space agencies are working together on a new type of telescope. The James Webb Space Telescope (JWST) will detect infrared radiation instead of visible light, which will allow it to see even further into the distant Universe. It is intended for launch in 2014 and will orbit the Sun in a similar way to Earth, but about 1.5 million kilometres (almost 1 million miles) from our planet. The JWST's main mirror will be made of 18 folded, gold-coated segments, which are designed to unfold in space. This is another new challenge for space engineers.

## Solar nuclear reactor

The Sun's energy is caused by nuclear fusion – the joining together of the nuclei of atoms. The inside of the Sun is so hot and dense that hydrogen gas turns into helium, giving off enormous amounts of energy. We now know that the Sun formed about 4.6 billion years ago and has used up about half of the hydrogen in its core. So the Sun should keep shining as it does now for about another 5 billion years. Then it will turn into a red giant, burning helium instead of hydrogen.

This nuclear fusion reactor is being tested at a research institute in Germany. Such reactors might be used to produce much of our energy in the future.

*fusion* joining of the nuclei of atoms causing the release of huge amounts of energy

# The Benefits of Space Exploration

Space exploration has given us many practical benefits. As well as increasing scientific knowledge, it has created many jobs all over the world. Among the biggest space agencies, NASA employs more than 18,600 people, ESA has about 2,000 employees, and CNES has more than 2,400.

## Agencies and private industry

In 2010 experts estimated the total world budget for space exploration to be about $45 billion. The United States has by far the biggest budget, at two fifths of the world total.

## International space exploration budgets

| Nation/continent | Space agency | Budget in billions of U.S. dollars |
|---|---|---|
| USA | NASA (National Aeronautics and Space Administration) | 18.7 |
| Europe | ESA (European Space Agency) | 4.9 |
| Russia | Roscosmos (Russian Federal Space Agency) | 2.7 |
| Japan | JAXA (Japan Aerospace Exploration Agency) | 2.6 |
| France | CNES (National Center of Space Research) | 1.0 |

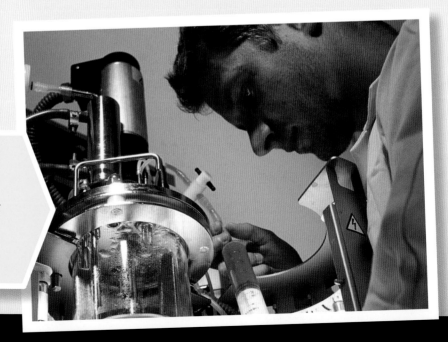

This scientist works for a European Space Agency project. He is testing new sources of food to be eaten by astronauts in space.

Thousands of different companies supply parts and technology to space agencies, which provide many more people with a living. In years to come, the use of private companies will increase, as national agencies try to keep their costs and workforce numbers down.

## Space tourism

Between 2001 and 2009, seven people visited the International Space Station as private, paying individuals. They are the world's first space tourists, though they prefer to be called "independent astronauts" or "private space explorers." Some carried out scientific experiments during their mission. The company Space Adventures is planning further tourist missions, including **suborbital** trips that are much less expensive.

## How much to travel in space?

"Since the dawn of time, man has dreamed of traveling to space and gazing back on the beauty of Earth. Now, that opportunity is closer than ever for private citizens thanks to the current development of suborbital spaceflight vehicles. Private individuals will be able to take the voyage of a lifetime into space, and do so at a relatively affordable price." That price starts at $102,000.

**Space Adventures website, 2010**

SpaceShipTwo (the middle craft) is designed to be launched into space from two linked aircraft. It will carry 2 pilots and 6 passengers.

## The blue planet

Seeing Earth from space has made people look at our planet in a different way. It has given us more of an idea of our place in the solar system, galaxy, and Universe. At the same time, seeing our beautiful blue planet has helped us appreciate how fragile it is.

## Satellite revolution

Since 1957 and Sputnik, artificial satellites have revolutionized life on Earth. More than 5,000 have been launched, though most have either stopped working or have burned up in the atmosphere. There are still more than 900 operational satellites circling our planet. Some are used for scientific research, collecting data about the atmosphere and making astronomical observations. Others observe and chart Earth's resources. Special satellites are used for weather forecasting, communications, and navigation. Spy satellites are mostly used for military purposes.

## Weather forecasting

The first weather satellite was launched in 1960. Called TIROS-I, it was 56 centimeters (22 inches) high and 107 centimeters (42 inches) wide. It contained two television cameras and two tape recorders that stored photographs when the satellite was out of communications range. TIROS was successful, but operated for just 77 days. Today's weather satellites are much more complex, with instruments that measure cloud cover, surface conditions such as ice and snow, atmospheric temperature, and ozone distribution. They also carry search and rescue instruments, which can detect distress signals from ships and planes.

This photograph of the Moon's surface and the Earth beyond was taken in 1968 from *Apollo 8*. Astronaut Jim Lovell said, "It makes you realize just what you have back there on Earth."

Satellite images allow emergency services to track and observe the spread of wildfires (the red patches).

## Observing the Earth

Earth observation satellites have become more important in recent years. They can be used to find mineral deposits, freshwater supplies, and even sources of pollution. Satellites can also watch how ecosystems respond to change. In recent years, a great deal of satellite and computer power has been used to monitor global warming, especially in the polar regions. Satellites can also observe and record large-scale natural disasters. This data and photographic information can help us understand these events more clearly, as well as help emergency services respond better to the catastrophe.

### *Fighting wildfires*

Satellite images are used to record, track, and predict the paths of dangerous forest fires. In 2007, NASA rapid response images (special satellite images that can be used only a few hours after being taken) were extremely useful to the authorities in Southern California when wildfires raged from Santa Barbara county to the U.S.– Mexico border.

## Satellite navigation

In 2010, a manufacturer of satellite navigation (satnav) systems advertised its products this way. "Satellite navigation brings Space Age technology into your daily life. Forget paper maps: through the wonders of the Global Positioning System (GPS), you can sit at the wheel of your car and be guided from A to B with the aid of a machine the size of a pack of playing cards. The new portable satnav units work 'straight-out-of-the-box': just buy one, put it in your car, and away you go."

## A world of communication

Communications satellites have had a huge effect on our daily lives. They act as receiving and transmitting stations for radio signals. Most are in a **geosynchronous** orbit, which means that the satellite circles Earth at the same speed as the planet spins on its axis. The satellite stays fixed over a base station on the ground. Communications satellites have increased the use and range of television and radio broadcasts, telephones, and Internet connections. Journalists and others use satellite and video phones to be in direct communication with the rest of the world from remote locations.

## Global positioning

The Global Positioning System (GPS) uses satellites to provide location information to vehicles on Earth. The system is very useful to ships, planes, and road vehicles. In recent years, it has been used in private cars and smartphones, providing satellite navigation. Many drivers have become so used to being told by their onboard GPS computer how to get to their destination that they would be lost without it.

Satnav systems can offer drivers a choice of routes and guide them to their destination. They can follow the map and listen to instructions.

Voice-controlled wheelchairs, communication systems, and computers have all developed with help from space research.

## Advances in health care

Space exploration has led to medical developments that can benefit us all. Some examples include:

- Surgical laser. A special laser was developed to examine the ozone layer. Modern surgeons use the technology to help clear patients' blood vessels.

- Cool suit. Space suits have a liquid cooling garment next to the astronaut's skin, to control body temperature. The system is now used to help patients with serious illnesses, especially by lowering their temperature.

- Programmable heart pacemaker. Computer technology developed for NASA spaceships is used in an electrical device that gives small shocks to the heart to make it beat more regularly.

- Artificial heart. Space shuttle fuel pumps led to the development of a tiny device that can be successfully implanted into human patients.

- Voice-controlled wheelchair. Robot technology developed by NASA for use in space is used to respond to 35 different voice commands from wheelchair users.

- Infrared thermometer. First developed to measure the temperature of distant stars and planets, this is now used on Earth as an extremely accurate hand-held thermometer.

- Cancer check. Work on reducing the cost of a digital imaging system for use in space led to its use in checking for breast cancer and avoiding the need for surgery.

### From moons to brains

Magnetic Resonance Imaging (MRI) is used for brain scans and producing images of muscles and internal organs. It is very useful to doctors in diagnosing illness. This form of medical scanning was not invented by space scientists, but they did develop a way of enhancing digital images of the Moon. This helped lead to the introduction of MRI techniques.

# Space Products for Everyday Use

Space research has led to the production of all sorts of different merchandise in a variety of fields. Many of these products have found a use in our everyday lives that is quite different from their use in space. Space programs have also helped develop or raise people's awareness of existing technologies or ideas.

## Computer technology

Space explorers have needed and used computers throughout the Space Age. Success would not have been possible without them. The biggest developments in computing since the 1950s have been an enormous increase in power and an equally large decrease in size. In the United States, NASA developed a computerized scheduling system that manages all the thousands of activities involved in launching a spaceship. The system, which uses artificial intelligence, was then licensed to a company for commercial use. NASA has also been involved in the development of **virtual reality** devices.

This diagram shows the main control panel of an Apollo command module (the main part of the spacecraft). It gives us an idea of how complex space flight is. We learned a great deal through the development of technology like this.

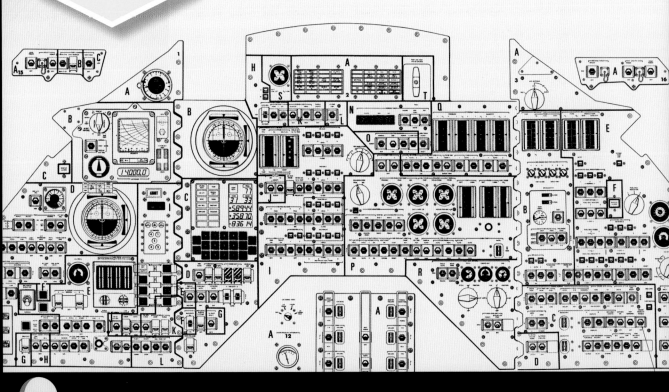

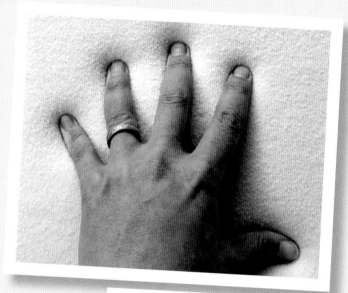

The useful material called memory foam can mold itself quickly to the shape that presses on it.

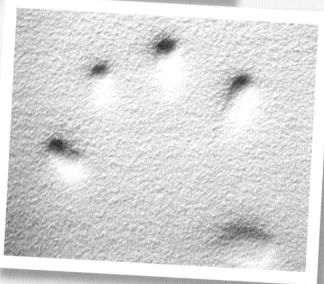

## Non-stick pans

The idea that the non-stick surface called Teflon was a product of space exploration is a myth. The substance with the scientific name poly-tetrafluoroethylene was actually discovered in 1938 by the U.S. chemist Roy Plunkett. NASA later gave great publicity to Teflon by applying it to heat shields and space suits. In the same way, the space program became associated with the Velcro hook-and-loop fastener, which was invented in 1941 by Swiss engineer George de Mestral. Velcro was very useful for anchoring equipment in the zero gravity of space.

## Memory foam

In the 1960s and 1970s, NASA scientists developed a special kind of plastic foam that increased the safety and comfort of aircraft seats. Originally called slow spring-back foam, this material was then used in medical equipment and sports helmets. It became known as memory foam, and in the 1980s was first used in mattresses. It was particularly useful for hospital patients. Since then, the foam has become less expensive and is now used more widely for mattresses and pillows, as well as saddles for horse-riders and motorcyclists. The company that makes memory foam now appears in the U.S. Space Foundation's Space Technology Hall of Fame.

A Russian cosmonaut tries out a new space suit in Houston, Texas. The special suit was specially developed for working outside the International Space Station.

## Faster swimsuits

Space engineers at the Langley Research Center in Virginia developed a system of aerodynamic "riblets." These are tiny grooves in airplane and spaceship surfaces that reduce air friction to improve flight smoothness and speed. The system works with water as well as air, and was later applied to the surfaces of rowing and sailing boats. When they were tested on racing swimsuits, the grooves were found to increase swimmers' speeds by as much as 15 percent.

## Consumer products

Space research and development has led to many well-known products, including the following:

- Scratch-resistant lenses. A special process developed by NASA coats lenses with a film of carbon. This is very useful for eyeglasses and sunglasses.

- Sports shoes. A material that was developed for astronauts' Moon boots was then used in the soles of sports shoes. It made them more stable and improved their shock absorption.

- Exercise machines. Special exercisers have been developed for astronauts, to improve their heart and muscle performance (see page 8). The astronaut stands or lies on the machine to exercise arms and legs. The machine was then adapted for sports-club and home use.

- Water purification. A system using silver–copper electrodes was first used to sterilize water on long space flights. The system was then transferred to swimming pools to kill bacteria and algae without the use of chemicals.

- Golf balls. Space engineers have done a lot of work on aerodynamics technology, and their research led to a newly designed golf ball. It has 500 dimples arranged in a pattern of 60 triangles, which make the ball fly faster and further.

## Transportation safety

Space research has led to many new developments in airplane safety. For example, work on de-icers led to improvement in the anti-icing systems used on airplanes before they take off in freezing conditions. This has improved safety enormously, because ice on an airplane's wings reduces lift. Research on composite materials for spaceships has led to improvements in helicopters, increasing fuselage strength and reducing weight. The materials are made by combining more than one substance, such as different plastics. Composites also make better, safer brake linings for trucks and cars. Space research has helped contribute to the development of improved jet engines in aircraft, which are quieter, use less fuel, and produce less pollution than previous versions.

Workers use a crane to spray an aircraft with de-icing fluid at Chicago's O'Hare International Airport.

# International Cooperation

Since the end of the space race and the Cold War, there has been increasing international cooperation in space exploration. Individual nations have realized that they have much to gain by joining together and much to lose if they waste energy and resources on unnecessary rivalry. The best example of cooperative effort is the International Space Station (ISS) project, which began fully in 1993.

## Space laboratory

The ISS is a joint project by space agencies from Brazil, Canada, Europe, Japan, Russia, and the United States. By the time it was ten years old, 20 different sections had been added to the station and more than 160 astronauts had visited it from various nations. The station is scheduled to be completed by 2011 and is expected to remain in operation until 2020. By 2010 the ISS had already orbited the Earth nearly 67,000 times. By then it was 88 meters (289 feet) long and 109 meters (358 feet) wide. Its main purpose is as a research laboratory, where long-term scientific studies can be conducted. These include the effects on the human body of spending a long time in space.

A U.S. astronaut disconnects cables outside a new module of the International Space Station.

## European Space Agency (ESA)

The European share of the ISS is made up of space agencies from Belgium, Denmark, France, Germany, Italy, Netherlands, Norway, Spain, Sweden, and Switzerland. ESA was founded in 1975 and has its headquarters in Paris, France. Its space center and launch pads are in Kourou, French Guiana, and mission control is in Darmstadt, Germany. This truly international organization has close ties with other space agencies around the world.

## The purpose of ESA

"Today space activities are pursued for the benefit of citizens, and citizens are asking for a better quality of life on Earth. They want greater security and economic wealth, but they also want to pursue their dreams, to increase their knowledge, and they want younger people to be attracted to the pursuit of science and technology. I think that space can do all of this: it can produce a higher quality of life, better security, more economic wealth, and also fulfil our citizens' dreams and thirst for knowledge, and attract the young generation."

"Through ESA, we can help make 'our spaceship,' the Earth, a better place to live in."

**Jean-Jacques Dordain, Director General of the European Space Agency, 2007 (1st quote), 2010 (2nd quote)**

An artist's impression of ESA's twin BepiColumbo spacecraft orbiting Mercury. Launch is planned to take place in 2014, and the craft will take six years to reach Mercury.

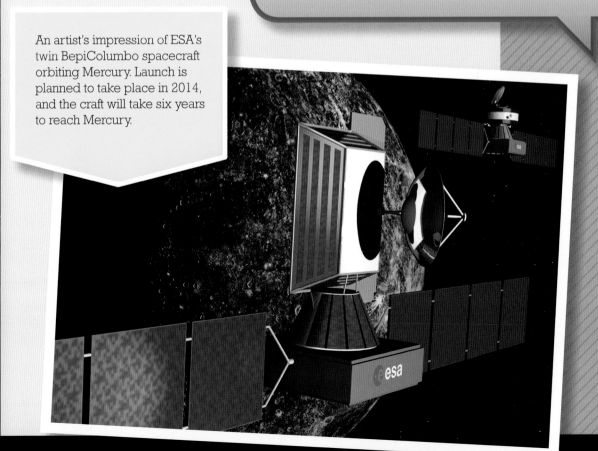

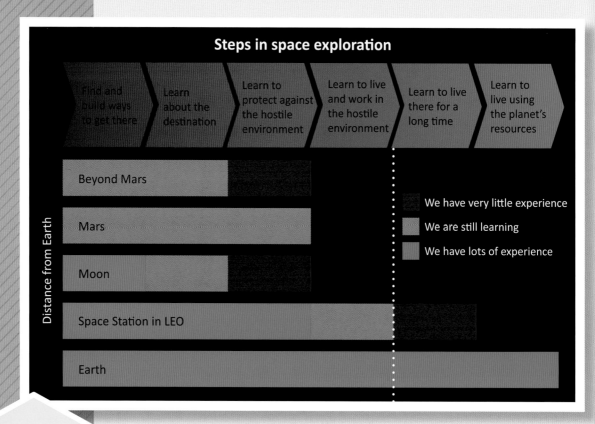

The diagram shows our experience of living in space. We have to reach the dotted line in order to be able to live in a particular place. LEO stands for Low Earth Orbit, the path of the International Space Station.

## Global Exploration Strategy

In 2007, a group of fourteen space agencies, including ESA and NASA, published a Global Exploration Strategy. They proposed a coordinated plan of exploring the space around the Earth, Moon, and Mars, which they all agreed were places where humans will one day live and work. The diagram shows how far we have progressed in this aim.

## Who owns the Moon?

One of the greatest advantages of international cooperation in space is that it helps avoid any territorial claims. The Outer Space Treaty of 1967, which has been signed by 125 countries, forbids any country or group from claiming territory in space. It states that all space resources are the "common heritage of mankind." Your heritage is your history and belongings, so this means that space resources belong to everyone equally. No one is allowed to claim rulership over space. So no country or group of people can own the Moon or any part of it. These laws were developed and are enforced by the International Institute of Space Law, which is based in Paris, France.

## Lunar outpost

Twelve U.S. Apollo astronauts walked on the Moon between 1969 and 1972. Now NASA is working on a project to build a colony on the Moon between 2019 and 2024. The aim of the Lunar Outpost program is for groups of four astronauts to visit the Moon and help build up a colony. This might then be used for a future venture to Mars. It has been reported that the Japanese and Chinese space agencies are also working on programs to build lunar bases. Most experts agree that it will be much better for Earth's people if the projects become truly international. Other people believe that a new kind of space race will push the boundaries of technology, science, and exploration further and quicker.

## Serving society through space exploration

"In the future, a sustained but affordable agenda of globally coordinated space exploration can serve society through:
- securing new knowledge and solving global challenges in space and on Earth through innovative technology;
- permanently extending human presence into space, physically and culturally;
- enabling economic expansion and new business opportunities;
- creating global partnerships by sharing challenging and peaceful goals;
- and inspiring society through collective effort and personal endeavor."

**Global Exploration Strategy, 2007**

An artist's impression of what a colony on the Moon might look like. Solar panels provide power for the inflatable structures.

# The Cost of Space Exploration

Many people believe that the biggest drawback to space exploration is cost. It is of course extremely expensive to run a space agency, sending rockets and spaceships into space, as well as continuously funding new research projects. Critics of space programs argue that such vast sums of money would be much better spent on useful projects on Earth. Such projects might include health care, education, and international aid aimed at reducing poverty in developing countries.

### Budgeting for space

NASA is the biggest space agency in the world. In the 21st century, the percentage of the total United States budget spent on NASA has gone down, from 0.75 percent in 2000, to 0.5 percent in 2010. It is still an enormous amount of money, however — a budget of $18.7 billion in 2010. This compares with $664 billion for the Department of Defense (35 times as much as NASA). Four times as much is spent on the Departments of Transportation and Health, and 2.5 times as much on Housing and Education.

The European Space Agency's budget is less than half as much as the European Union (a separate organization) spends on its own administration. The EU's budget for "preservation and management of natural resources" is 16 times bigger than ESA's total budget.

A woman carries a bag of rice in Port-au-Prince, Haiti, following the 2010 earthquake disaster. The U.S. foreign aid budget for 2010 was $37 billion, almost twice the size of NASA's budget.

An Apollo-17 astronaut checks the Lunar Rover on the Moon in 1972. This was the final Apollo lunar-landing mission.

## Expensive Apollo

The Apollo lunar project lasted from 1961 to 1975. In 1966, NASA's share of the US budget was 5.5 percent, its highest point and 11 times more than today. Experts have estimated that more than 400,000 people were involved in the Apollo project, and that the whole program cost $149 billion (in 2010 dollars). That is eight times the current annual budget.

## Satellites or libraries?

According to the Physics and Ethics Education Project (funded by the UK Institute of Physics), it costs about one billion dollars to develop and launch a satellite. The Project says this compares with:

- $60 million to build a new high school
- $400 million to build a university hospital
- $500 million to run a university hospital for a year
- $700 million for a civic center, health center, library, and shopping mall
- $1.5 billion to build the new Wembley Stadium, London
- $3.3 billion (estimated) to stage the 2012 Olympic Games in London
- $4.2 billion to build Terminal 5 at Heathrow Airport, London

### Why spend money on space exploration?

"Why spend money on NASA at all? Why spend money solving problems in space when we don't lack for problems to solve here on the ground? ... But for pennies on the dollar, the space program has fueled jobs and entire industries. For pennies on the dollar, the space program has improved our lives, advanced our society, strengthened our economy, and inspired generations of Americans."

**President Barack Obama, April 15, 2010**

## Defending the high cost of space exploration

NASA administrator Mike Griffin tells a story about the need to explain space connections: "I was once briefing a member of our own Congress when I was asked: 'Why do we need all these weather satellites when all we need to do is turn on the Weather Channel?' So I had to make the connection between the Weather Channel and weather satellites."

**New Scientist magazine, October 1, 2008**

## How much to launch a space shuttle?

NASA says it costs $450 million to launch a shuttle. The organization says that the shuttle *Endeavour*, which first flew in 1992, cost a total of $1.7 billion (one tenth of the current annual budget). It has flown on 24 missions.

Space Shuttle *Atlantis* stands on a mobile platform beside the launch pad at Kennedy Space Center, Florida, in 2006. The shuttle had to be moved because of the threat of a tropical storm before take-off.

The crew module of the *Orion* spaceship goes through tests at a NASA research center. The craft will carry as many as six astronauts.

## Yes or no to Constellation?

Early in the 21st century, the United States decided to build on the Apollo program and return astronauts to the Moon by 2020. The new program, called Constellation, would also include the building of a new spaceship, named *Orion*. This would visit asteroids and eventually, by 2030, the planet Mars. However, in 2009 U.S. politicians began to question this huge new space exploration program because of the cost. Critics of the program said it was much too expensive. Supporters, on the other hand, said establishing a new presence on the Moon would make further exploration cheaper. One of them, former astronaut and first man on the Moon Neil Armstrong, said in 2010: "A return to the moon would be the most productive path to expanding the human presence in the solar system." The debate has also centered on how much private companies should be involved in funding future programs such as this.

### One cup of coffee per person per year

"The cost of the ISS [International Space Station], including development, assembly and running costs over a period of at least 10 years, will come to 100 billion Euros [about $123 billion in 2010]. High technology on the space frontier is not cheap. However, the good news is that it comes cheaper than you might think. That 100 billion figure is shared over a period of almost 30 years between all the participants: the United States, Russia, Canada, Japan, and 10 of the 17 European nations who are part of ESA. The European share, at around 8 billion Euros [$10 billion] spread over the whole program, amounts to just one Euro spent by every European every year: less than the price of a cup of coffee in most of our big cities."

**European Space Agency website, 2005**

# Problems and Risks

All forms of human exploration involve problems and risks. Space exploration clearly presents dangers to astronauts and everyone else involved, since the explorers are constantly dealing with the unknown. If things go wrong during a space mission, it is very difficult to find ways to correct them.

## Space accidents

A memorial at the John F. Kennedy Space Center in Florida lists the names of the 24 U.S. astronauts who have died in accidents. Seventeen were lost in space accidents and seven died in airplane training and exercise accidents. Eight Russian cosmonauts have also been killed. The first of the three worst accidents took place on the Florida launch pad in 1967, when the *Apollo 1* capsule caught fire during a test, killing all three astronauts. There have also been two space shuttle disasters. In 1986, the shuttle *Challenger* broke up 73 seconds after lift-off, killing all seven on board. Then in 2003, the shuttle *Columbia* broke up on re-entering the Earth's atmosphere at the end of its mission, killing an additional seven astronauts.

Technicians check the Mars rover Spirit. The rover has a plaque commemorating the astronauts killed in the *Columbia* space shuttle disaster. Spirit successfully drove on Mars in 2004.

Brazilian technicians inspect what is left of the launch pad at Alcantara. The pad was severely damaged during the 2003 disaster that killed 21 people.

## What went wrong?

The shuttle program was stopped for two years following the *Columbia* accident, and construction of the International Space Station was put on hold. An investigation found that the problem was caused by a small piece of foam insulation that broke off the main fuel tank during blast-off. This damaged the front edge of the left wing of the shuttle, which then could not withstand the heat build-up during re-entry. *Columbia* was on its 28th mission.

## Star Wars

According to an international agreement signed by member states in 1976, space agencies agree to explore and use outer space for "peaceful purposes" only. However, a future space race or disagreement between powerful nations could lead to weapons being positioned or used in space. In 1983, the United States proposed a Strategic Defense Initiative, using satellite-mounted weapons to protect the country from any possible missile attack. The system was soon nicknamed Star Wars, and critics pointed out that the whole idea was extremely dangerous. In any case, it never worked properly and could have increased the likelihood of a nuclear accident or world war.

## Launch-pad explosion

On August 22, 2003, a Brazilian VLS-1 satellite-launching rocket exploded on the pad at Alcantara in northern Brazil, killing 21 workers, engineers, and scientists on the ground. The disaster happened when one of the rocket's four solid-fuel motors ignited accidentally. The Brazilian Space Agency successfully launched its first rocket, the VSB-30, a year later.

## Space junk

There are thousands of pieces of space junk orbiting the Earth. This "orbital debris" comes from old spaceships and satellites, pieces of launch vehicles, explosions, collisions, and even tiny flecks of paint. Some pieces were released deliberately as part of space missions. In 2007, a Chinese satellite deliberately destroyed another by colliding into it. According to experts, the official debris count from this anti-satellite missile test was 2,317 pieces that were big enough to be tracked. Clearly this junk poses a hazard to spaceships with or without human crews, and some pieces reach Earth without burning up.

## Satellite crash

On February 10, 2009, a working U.S. Iridium-33 satellite crashed into a Russian Cosmos-2251 satellite that was no longer in use. The crash happened at a height of 790 kilometers (490 miles) over Siberia. "This is the first time we've ever had two intact spaceship accidentally run into each other," said Nicholas Johnson, chief scientist of NASA's Orbital Debris Program Office. "It was a bad day for both of them."

This image is a computer-generated diagram used by NASA to show the orbital debris that is currently in low Earth orbit (LEO).

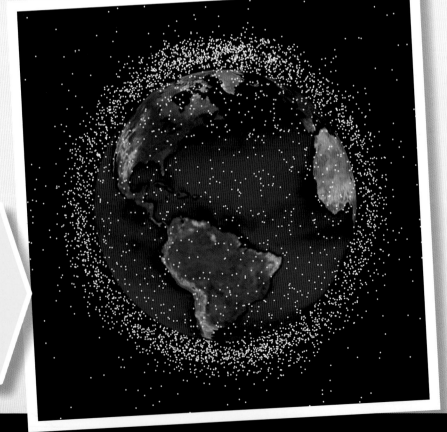

A Russian cosmonaut checks a plant in a growing experiment aboard the International Space Station. Scientists are interested in the effects of zero gravity on plant growth.

## Dealing with the unknown

Could there be a danger in exploring unknown parts of space? Some people have suggested that astronauts or robot spaceships might have contact with harmful substances, including microorganisms, that are not even known on Earth. Explorers could bring them back to their home planet without even realizing it. Experiments in space stations have shown that bacteria from Earth become more dangerous to humans in weightless conditions. This could mean that the further humans explore away from Earth, and the longer they stay in space, the greater the danger.

## Respect for the Universe

Environmentalists are concerned about the natural world and do everything they can to protect Earth's natural resources. You can argue that exactly the same principles should be applied to the rest of the Universe. People do not own space and should respect its timeless beauty. Many people certainly agree that humans should not harm the Universe or fill it with junk.

### How much orbital debris is currently in Earth orbit?

"Approximately 19,000 objects larger than 10 centimeters (almost 4 inches) are known to exist. The estimated population of particles between 1 and 10 centimeters (up to 4 inches) in diameter is approximately 500,000. The number of particles smaller than 1 cm probably exceeds tens of millions."

**NASA, 2009**

# The Future

What does the future hold for space exploration, and what will its successes and failures do for us? Much will depend on the answers to questions raised by past missions. The biggest question must be: "Is space exploration a waste of money?" Present and future generations will have to answer that question. Currently, it seems likely that space missions will continue. Many missions are already planned, and the planet Mars seems to be the most popular goal.

## China heads for Mars

In 2003, China launched an astronaut into space, to become the third country to do so independently (after Soviet Russia and the United States). The China National Space Administration (CNSA) is aiming to send astronauts to the Moon by 2024. By then an unmanned mission to Mars is also planned, followed by Chinese astronauts flying to Mars around 2050. Chinese scientists have also mentioned Saturn as a long-term aim.

A Chinese astronaut leaves the *Shenzhou-6* capsule after orbiting Earth for five days in 2005. A two-man crew made China's second human space flight.

## Terraforming

Scientists are looking at ways to **terraform** other planets in order to be able to colonize them. This means transforming the planets so that they can support human life. Most scientists consider Mars to be the best candidate for terraforming. Basic requirements include water and energy sources. Plant life could be taken to Mars, and this would create oxygen so that further life could live on the planet.

## Near-Earth objects

A great deal of research is being done on near-Earth objects (NEOs), which are comets and asteroids that enter the Earth's region of space. Scientists are searching for ways to stop large NEOs from colliding with the Earth. Experts believe that large asteroids strike Earth once every few hundred thousand years, causing global disaster. Knowledge in this area is seen as another potential benefit of space research.

## India and the Sun

The Indian Space Research Organisation (ISRO) plans to launch a solar investigation satellite by 2012. Called Aditya (the word for "Sun" in the Sanskrit language), it will send back detailed information on our local star. ISRO sent an unmanned spaceship into lunar orbit in 2008. It plans to send an astronaut into space by 2015 and also has planned missions to Mars.

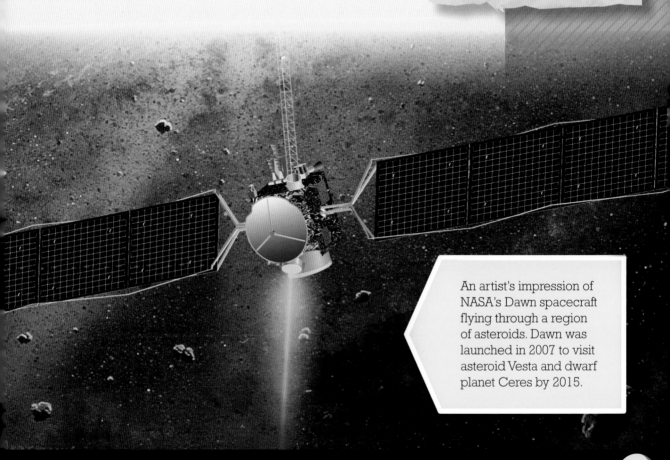

An artist's impression of NASA's Dawn spacecraft flying through a region of asteroids. Dawn was launched in 2007 to visit asteroid Vesta and dwarf planet Ceres by 2015.

## SETI

SETI stands for the Search for Extra-Terrestrial Intelligence (in other words, looking for life on other stars and planets in the Universe). In the past this has often meant flying saucers and strange-looking aliens, but it is also serious science. SETI will probably become even more serious in the future. In recent years several Earth-like planets have been identified close to distant stars. They could contain life in some form.

The dish of the enormous Arecibo radio telescope, in the mountains of Puerto Rico, is 305 meters (1,001 feet) across. The telescope is used for SETI projects, both sending and hoping to receive signals.

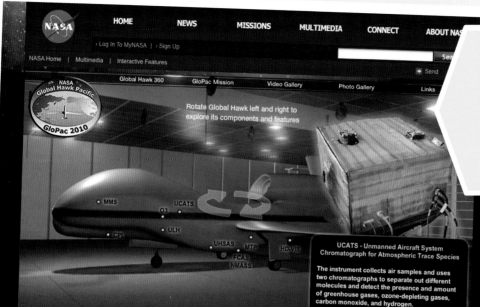

The NASA website (see page 46) has lots of interactive features, including animations and videos. These give us hands-on information about space exploration.

# Opinion polls

In 2009, CBS and Gallup published the following results to U.S. opinion polls:

- Has the space program brought enough benefits to justify its costs?
  *Yes: 58%. No: 38%*
- Should spending on the U.S. space program be increased or reduced?
  *Increased: 14%. Reduced: 30%. Maintained: 46%. Ended: 8%*
- Are you for sending astronauts to Mars?
  *Yes: 51%. No: 43%*

How would you answer the questions?

## Virtual presence

In the future we will be able to follow space missions on our computers, with live webcams and commentaries. Already space programs have simulated missions, so that Internet users can imagine what it is like to ride in a spaceship or walk on the Moon. The Global Exploration Strategy agreed by the world's major space agencies states that this new technology will make us all feel more positively towards space exploration. What do you think?

## Involving people

"Compared with the early days of lunar exploration, the more sophisticated media of today will create novel means to relate the space exploration journey to all people. Anyone may be able to participate personally in lunar robotic and human missions through virtual-presence technologies. In particular, children can be involved and will be inspired to become the explorers of the future — as scientists, engineers, teachers, and entrepreneurs."

**The Global Exploration Strategy, 2007**

# Timeline

**1957** Soviet Sputnik-1, the first human-made satellite, orbits Earth; Sputnik-2 carries a dog, Laika, into orbit.

**1958** Explorer-1, the first U.S. satellite in orbit, discovers Earth's radiation belt.

**1959** Luna-3 orbits the Moon and photographs the far side.

**1960** Tiros-1 is the first successful weather satellite.

**1961** *Vostok-1* carries Russian cosmonaut Yuri Gagarin, the first man in space; *Freedom-7* carries U.S. astronaut Alan Shepard into space.

**1962** U.S. Telstar-1 satellite transmits the first live transatlantic TV broadcast.

**1964** U.S. Ranger-7 sends close-up photos of the Moon.

**1965** U.S. Mariner-4 sends photos of Mars.

**1966** U.S. Lunar Orbiter 1 takes the first photo of Earth from the distance of the Moon.

**1967** Venera-4 sends data on the atmosphere of Venus.

**1968** *Apollo 8* is the first manned spaceship to orbit the Moon.

**1969** *Apollo 11's* Neil Armstrong and Edwin Aldrin become the first humans to walk on the Moon.

**1970** *Apollo 13* suffers an explosion but the crew return safely to Earth.

**1971** Soviet Salyut-1 space station is launched; U.S. Mariner-9 orbits Mars and maps its surface.

**1973** U.S. Mariner-10 sets off to photograph Venus and Mercury.

**1975** U.S. Apollo and Soviet *Soyuz-19* make the first international docking in space.

**1976** U.S. Viking-1 lands on Mars and tests the surface.

**1981** The first U.S. space shuttle mission, *Columbia*, is launched.

**1982** Venera-13 lands on Venus and analyzes the surface.

**1983** Space shuttle *Columbia* carries the ESA Spacelab-1 into orbit.

**1985** Japanese Sakigake probe and ESA Giotto craft are launched to Halley's Comet.

**1986** Soviet space station Mir is launched.

**1989** Shuttle *Atlantis* launches the Galileo spaceship towards Jupiter.

**1990** Shuttle *Discovery* launches the Hubble Space Telescope.

**1991** Shuttle *Columbia* carries Spacelab SLS-1, to investigate the effects of weightlessness on humans.

**1995** Cosmonaut Valeri Polyakov returns to Earth after a record-breaking 438-day mission aboard space station Mir.

**1997** NEAR (Near Earth Asteroid Rendezvous) probe passes asteroid Mathilde on its way to asteroid 433-Eros; Pathfinder lands on Mars with roving robot Sojourner.

**1998** The first component of the International Space Station is launched by a Russian rocket.

**1999** China launches its first Shenzhou spaceship.

**2001** U.S. businessman Dennis Tito pays a reported $20 million to become the first space tourist aboard a Soyuz spaceship and the ISS.

**2004** *SpaceShipOne* is launched from an aircraft to make the first independently funded space flight.

**2005** Cassini spaceship drops Huygens probe onto the surface of Saturn's moon Titan.

**2006** Samples from Comet Wild 2 return to Earth in the U.S. Stardust capsule.

**2010** Last flight of U.S. shuttle *Endeavour*; first flight of X-37B unmanned robotic spaceship.

# Glossary

**astronomer**  scientist who studies space and everything in it

**atmosphere**  blanket of gases that surrounds a planet such as Earth

**Big Bang**  theory that the Universe started with a tiny point about 13.5 billion years ago and has been expanding ever since

**Big Crunch**  theory that the Universe will eventually stop expanding and collapse to nothing again

**coma**  cloud of gas and dust around the nucleus of a comet

**comet**  mass of ice and dust with a tail of gas that moves around the solar system

**fusion**  joining of the nuclei of atoms of light elements under pressure, releasing huge amounts of energy. The fusion of hydrogen nuclei to make helium is what makes stars shine.

**galaxy**  group of billions of stars, gas, and dust bound together by gravity. Our own galaxy is the Milky Way.

**geosynchronous**  describing the orbit of a satellite that moves at the same speed as the Earth's spin and so stays above the same spot

**gravity**  force that attracts things towards the center of Earth (or another planet, star, or galaxy)

**infrared** describing radiation waves from the Sun that have more energy than radio waves but less energy than visible light or X-rays

**nucleus** solid center of a comet's head

**orbit** path that a satellite or other object follows around an object such as a star or planet

**satellite** natural or human-made object that orbits a planet; a moon is a natural satellite

**solar system** our Sun and all the planets and moons that move around it

**suborbital** not making a complete orbit of the Earth

**telescope** instrument that makes distant objects, such as planets and stars, appear much nearer and bigger

**terraform** to transform a planet so that it is able to support human life

**Universe** all of space and everything contained in it

**virtual reality** computer-generated simulation of a real environment that can be interacted with in a real or physical way

# Find Out More

## Books

Couper, Heather, and Nigel Henbest. *DK Encyclopedia of Space.* New York, NY: DK Publishing, 2009.

Hartman, Eve, and Wendy Meshbesher. *Mission to Mars.* Chicago, IL: Raintree, 2011.

Rooney, Anne. *Earth's Final Frontiers: Outer Space.* Chicago, IL: Heinemann Library, 2008.

Solway, Andrew. *Can We Travel to the Stars? Space Flight and Space Exploration.* Chicago, IL: Heinemann Library, 2006.

## Websites

**www.nasa.gov**
The NASA website has fascinating details of all its missions, including future plans. In the multimedia section, there are videos, podcasts, and interactive features.

**http://spaceflight.nasa.gov/shuttle/benefits/index.html**
NASA's view on space shuttle benefits.

**www.esa.int**
The European Space Agency provides features on life in space, expanding frontiers, improving daily life, protecting the environment, and benefits for Europe.

**www.spacetechhalloffame.org**
The Space Foundation's Hall of Fame honors those who "quietly transform technology originally developed for space exploration into products that help improve the quality of life here on Earth."

## Topics to investigate

There are many different topics related to space exploration and the question of what it does for us. The websites on the previous page might give some interesting leads. Here are some further research ideas.

### NASA spinoffs

*Spinoff* is a NASA publication featuring space technology that has led to successful commercial products. It is part of the NASA Innovative Partnerships Program, which they say "benefits global competition and the economy." The online version of *Spinoff* (**www.sti.nasa.gov/tto**) gives detailed information on some of the innovations mentioned in this book, plus many more.

### SETI at home

SETI@home is a project using home computers to help search for extraterrestrial intelligence. It is run by the University of California and is funded by grants from the National Science Foundation, NASA, and personal donations. Like other SETI projects, it uses radio telescopes to listen for signals from space. These could provide evidence of other life in the Universe. The project uses the enormous computer power provided by all of us at home. For more details, visit **http:// setiathome.berkeley.edu**. If you want to consider taking part, make sure you read the rules and policies page first.

### Energy sources

Learn more about energy sources in space and on Earth. Solar energy is vitally important, and solar sails could be used more on future space missions. Nuclear-powered rockets and spaceships are another possibility. The use of nuclear energy is controversial, with strong views for and against. Ion engines work by the power of electrical charges and are already being tested and used. You could investigate these three different forms of spaceship engines by looking at books and typing the terms into an Internet search engine. Or you could start by entering them in the search box of the NASA website.

# Index